The Keen English Idiom Master:

250 Important Hand-Picked Idiomatic
Expressions and Words Used In Everyday Life

The Keen English Idiom Master:

250 Important Hand-Picked Idiomatic Expressions and Words Used In Everyday Life

by

Charles Joseph Smith

NOTE FROM THE AUTHOR

The inspiration for writing this book was this – I was studying for the SAT test in the mid-1980s, trying to study as much vocabulary as I could so I could ace the test especially in the vocabulary sections and get a perfect score of 1600 and this would get me easily into college, while being under the spectrum of autism giving me an extra advantage. Sadly, after taking the test despite my aforementioned , I ended up in the mid-300s in points on Math and Verbal, and only got about a 700 total in the tests. I was pretty disappointed.

So, from this pseudo-failure, I decided to learn more vocabulary – and idiomatic expressions, to better myself as a person and a thinker, and after listening to scores of movies, news programs, sporting events, TV talk shows and other events, I realized in my hunches that there were idiomatic expressions and words coming from slang that everyday people will need to know, even if they know the English language at a basic fluency level in listening and reading.

From this book, I only hope that I can contribute the helping of enriching the reader more deeply into the English language, and moreover, inspire the reader to keep oneself updated on other idioms that one can understand in context, whether it was used in the past, or just recently, and for this, I hope this help will be made just for you.

---Charles Joseph Smith

LIST OF ABBREVIATIONS

adj. – adjective

adv. - adverb

colloq. - colloquial

colloq. n. – colloquial noun

colloq. p. – colloquial phrase

interj. - interjection

n. - noun

n.p. – noun phrase

prep. - preposition

prep. n. – prepositional noun

prep. p. – prepositional phrase

v. – verb

v. p. – verb phrase

1. air defense (n. p.)--refers to hand-held or fixed anti-aircraft weapons used in war, such as surface-to-air missiles

2. at cost (p.p.)--means an item is priced as is, without any markups

3. B.O. (n.)--body odor

4. back-to-back (adj.)--means the backs of two persons touching each other or very close to each other.

(adj.)--two things happening successively (such as two home runs)

5. back-to-back-to-back (adj.)--means three things happening successively (such as three home runs)

6. bad-mouth (v. p.)--using obscene or vulgar language

7. ballyard (n.)--a ballpark; a baseball stadium or arena

8. barbecue (v.)--to let something set on fire; to be exposed to extreme heat or fire; to be killed. Also: **be toast (v.)**

9. baseline (n.)--the area where the end of the horizontal, long boundary ends and the vertical, short boundary begins

10. beat (n.)--a break-dance drum track or sample

11. behind closed doors (prep. p.)--this refers to something that can be divulged despite the milieu of secrecy, privacy, or confidentiality existing.

12. belle (n.)--French for "beautiful", it often refers to a lady in old times (or even a "sweetheart" as well). An example of a "belle" is a beautiful rustic girl in the white silken dress.

13. big ones (pl. n.)--American dollars

14. black out (v. p.)--to pass out; to lose conciousness

15. blast (n.)--a great event; an explosive sight; a successful happening

16. bloodbath (n.)--a slaughterhouse; an area where a mass-murder or massacre is taking place

17. blow (v.) --To explode into rage, usually uncontrollably.

      (v.) – To detonate; to explode; to burst

18. bomb (n.)--A failure; a flop; a fiasco.

      (n.)--Something that was expected to be successful but it turns awfully bad.

      (v.)--To explode (or detonate); to explode (or detonate) a device or bomb.

19. boogie (v.)--to dance swing-style in freedom

20. boogie down (v. p.)--to dance freestyle to dance or dance-mix music

21. boot camp (n. p.) - A military-style camp where recruits are constantly given orders

and demanding physical workouts by drill sergeants.

22. booze (n.)--beer; wine; any alcoholic beverage

23. boys in blue (pl. n.)--cops; police; police officers

24. break (n.)--a situation where an offender runs free of the defense on the way to the other opponents' basket (basketball)

(n.) – in baseball, it is when the runner on the original base tries to run toward the next base to try to create a successful base steal

25. breaker (n.)--a break-dancer

26. brick (n.)--A thrown or catapulted object that misses its target mainly by ricocheting into the ground.

(n.)--In basketball, a missed free throw that bounces off high off the net vertically before falling down.

27. bring someone to its knees (v. p.)--make someone pay attention

28. brotha (n.)—brother

29. bucket (n.)--In basketball, a basket shot (or simply, a "shot").

30. by the busload (prep. p.)--a large grove of people

31. cakewalk (n.)--A type of 20th century American Negro dance possibly inspired by the minstrel milieu and was an offshoot (in musical form) to ragtime music.

(n.)--A easy walk-through something that was expected to cause another person great endurance or hardship.

32. caliente (adj.)--Spanish for "hot", it is often said of some Latin dances and/or music, especially mambo

33. can (v.)--To shout.

(v.)--To ostracize; to criticize with a negative slant.

34. can of corn (prep. p.)--In baseball, one fly ball that can be easily caught by an infielder or outfielder.

35. carnie (n.)--carnival; fair

36. Chambana (n.)--an unusual acronym (and portmanteau) for the twin towns of Champaign-Urbana, two famous college towns in Champaign County (in the state of Illinois).

37. chop shop (n. p.)--This is an illicit place where stolen vehicles are usually stripped of its valuable parts so that the stealers can sell them.

38. classic rock (n. p.)--American-style rock music from past days

39. cock (n.)--penis

40. come clean (v.)--to free oneself from suspicion or reprehensibility

41. con (n.)--abbreviation for convict

42. court-martialled (adj.)--Being on trial in a military-style court on a civil or criminal charge or charges.

       (adj.)--One facing or is obligated (usually by subpoena) to appear in a court-martial.

43. crack house (n.)--A place notoriously known for illicit drug dealing, selling, or making (especially of cocaine, crack cocaine, or "rock"). Also called **drug house.**

44. cross the line (prep. p.)--In the topic of sexual harrassment or sexual abuse/assault, it means to go beyond the limits of one's sexual boundaries or one's personal space.

45. cry foul (v.)--protest that something is wrong or unfair

46. cut it (v.)--To result in some degree of success.

(v.)--To do such a thing so as to create a win, success, or happiness (mainly by a result of effort).

47. day in and day out (colloq. p.)--every day; all-day

48. declassified (adj.)--This means that a file, document, or data that was usually confidential or classified was modified in such way that it can be accessed more publicly.

49. deadbeat (n.)--A person who is obligated to pay child support for his child or children but flagrantly or blatantly refuses to do so (either by moral standars or under the law), even under the threat or possiblility of lawsuit, arrest, or injunctive relief.

50. dead-end job (n. p.)--A job that an employee gets bored so much that the employee begins to loathe that job and want to move to a higher-paying job.

51. dicey (adj.)--chancy; risky

52. dinger (n.)--In baseball, a home run.

53. dollar anything (colloq.)--in a bar or tavern establishment, it means any beer, wine, or mixed liquor is $1

54. Doomsday clock (n. p.) This clock tells whether or not the United States is on the brink of a nuclear bomb attack (or annihilation). The risk of nuclear war becomes greater when the clock's hands goes nearer to midnight; the risk becomes less when it is moved away from midnight.

55. dope (n.)--An illicit drug.

(n.)--Illicit drugs.

56. double-dutch (adj.)--a type of jump rope technique where jump ropes (2 of them) go around in opposite directions

57. double-team (n. p.)—The act of surrounding an offensive player with 2 defensive players in man-to-man defense to try to steal the ball (this defensive tactic is used often in basketball).

58. double up (v. p.)—to create or make a double play. In baseball, this involves usually a right fielder's (or any other fielder's) throw to the first baseman to put out the runner who had run from first and tried to go back to first (assuming the fielder would not catch the ball), realizing too late that the ball was caught by the fielder, and fails to touch first base before the first baseman gets the ball and touches first base. Double plays occasionally occur this way.

59. down (adj.)--failed; not working; out of service

60. dram shop (n. p.)--This refers to the party host's threat of possible civil and/or criminal liablility if one allows any partyers who drink alcoholic beverages to be in situations which can cause damage, injury, or death to them or to other people (such as a fatal accident due to driving drunk). Also called **dram-shop liability.**

61. drive-by (n.)--short for drive-by shooting

62. drop (v.)--to lose a game

63. drop a line (v. p.)--to call; telephone

64. drop names (v. p.)--to divulge or call out names

65. drown in debt (v. p.)--to be very deep into debt; to be in the red; to default a lot in payments or loans

66. dude (n.)--A cool friend or buddy.

       (n.)--A friend; buddy; pal.

67. dusties (pl. n.)--refers to pop music of the past related to African-Americans, such as rhythm-and-blues and soul

68. evacuee (n.)--one who evacuates

69. ex (n.) Refers to a person formerly in love with a lover, who he or she loses usually by a breakup, divorce, or rejection. This word is often used in domestic cases or disputes.
(Sometimes, the "ex" is followed by a hyphen to a word of domestic relation, such as "ex-girlfriend".)

70. ex-con (n.)--a person who gets released after serving one's prison or jail sentence

71. ex-cop (n.)--a person who retired or was terminated from the police force

72. explode (v.)--to run hastily; to get angry suddenly

73. exposé (n.) This refers to a moment that allows for overt divulging of evidence for informing people on scams, schemes, deceptive activity, or even indecent behavior. This word is often jargon in news or investigative reporting.(It comes from the French verb "exposer", so literally, it means "exposed".)

74. fast-paced (adj.)--hurried; quick-thinking

75. Feds (n.)--Refers to the police, especially the police who work for the Federal Bureau of Investigation (FBI).

(n.)--A person or group to whom the criminal thinks he fears him. (For example, a drug dealer fears that the FBI is about to track him or her down.)

76. field goal (n. p.)--a 2-point or 3-point shot (basketball)

77. filibuster (n.) A Congressional technique involving so much negative conversation against a proposed bill to the point of being invaild or useless. It is known as "talking a bill to death."

78. first-of-its-kind (n.)--brand new; original; something not seen before

79. flash flood (n. p.)--a sudden, heavy rainstorm that triggers a flood afterwards, for the storm comes too fast for the soil or ground to absorb

80. flattop (n.)--A nickname for an aircraft carrier in the Navy, friend or enemy.

81. fly-by-night (adj.)--temporary, and usually not reputable (often said of a business or a firm)

82. follow (n.)--a back-up shot or second-effort shot that a player attempts after a rebound (basketball)

83. fork over (v. p .)--to give; to pay; to remit

84. foul play (n.) Criminal activity that involves a lost or missing person (living or dead).

(n.) In sports, any combative activity against the rules or regulations.

85. foul trouble (n.)--A situation where a player is dangerously close to getting a subsequent foul that can disqualify the player for the rest of the game. This phrase is often heard in basketball.

86. from downtown (n.) In basketball, a shot that is made outside the 3-point shot boundary, or a long distance shot.

(n.) In football, a very long pass from the quarterback to the receiver.(In this case, it is also known as "the long bomb.")

Note: There is a expression in baseball called **"to hit it downtown"**, which means that the batter hits a home run.

87. gas (n.)--Energy a person needs through food and/or drink.

(n.)--Gasoline; natural gas.

(n.)--In baseball, a fast ball that goes so fast that it forces a batter to swing at it, often resulting in a missed swing.

88. gas guzzler (n. p.)--often said of a vehicle that has the lowest miles-per-gallon rating

89. general skinny (n. p.)--same as the word 'lowdown'

90. get away with murder (v. p.)--This means to successfully avoid criminal prosecution or arrest after one commits murder or homicide. It can also mean that a person charged with murder while on trial is instead received a verdict of not guilty.

91. get the gates (v. p.)--to be kicked out; be ejected or expelled

92. get the pink slip (v. p.)--To be laid off from a job.

(v. p.)--To get a notice or letter informing of being laid off the job.

93. give and go (n.p.)--This basketball technique involves the offending player passing the ball (while he is being held by the defense) to a running player who is in a direct path to the basket, and then he shoots the ball to finish the play.

94. GLBT (abbrev.)--means Gay, Lesbian, Bisexual and Transgender.

95. golden years (pl. n.)--a human being's senior years; the time a human being reaches

late adulthood

96. go broke (v. p.)--to be poor; to be penniless

97. go dutch (v. p.)--to allow equal financial responsibility between 2 partners during a date

98. good stuff (n. p.)--in baseball, a good selection of pitches

99. graveyard shift (n. p.)--Usually, a worker who works at a time when most of the people in one's city, town, village or neighborhood are falling asleep.

100. gridlock (n.)--Refers to an encumbrance that keeps a person or vehicle from going smoothly.

       (n.) - Any gauntlet-like (or quasi-gauntlet) event or situation a person or animal has to endure.

101. gully-washer (n.)--a heavy rainstorm; a downpour; a deluge

102. gut-wrenchingly (adv.)--starkingly; strongly

103. hair-raising (adj.)--something that causes the raising of a person's hair, usually due to fright or surprise

104. hand jive (n.)--Inspired from the musical Grease, it is a type of fad dance (and a line dance) where people are in a crouching position and rapidly alternating hands on both knees as if the knees are like bongo drums.

105. hang whiff'em (colloq. n.) - In baseball, a line drive that goes very fast across the infield.

(colloq. n.) - In baseball, a fast ball that goes by the batter who attempts to swing at it but misses it.

106. hard time (n. p.) - A long prison or jail sentence, such as life imprisonment.

(n. p.) - Imprisonment which involves the convict doing some hard labor while in prison (such as doing some cultivation as part of a prison chain gang).

107. heads-up (adj.)--something done with a lot of attention or concentration (basketball)

108. heartthrob (n.)--famous star young people admire or look up to

109. high-stakes (adj.)--very risky; very chancy

110. hit (n.)--An assassination, or a plot (or conspiracy) leading to assassination, usually orchestrated by a hitman (or someone paid to commit a murder).

111. hit-and-run (coll. n. p.)-- In baseball, a runner who runs from one base tothe next (usually from first base to second) before the batter hits the ball, expecting a possible base hit.

(n.)--To hit a person in a vehicular accident and to leave the accident serious injury is involved)

112. hit pay dirt (v.)--to find something one really wanted dearly; to hit the jackpot; to win or earn a large amount of money

113. hit the three (v. p.)--to shoot a 3-point shot (basketball)

114. hoopla (n.)--haranguing; pandemonium; a lively craze; cheering

115. household name (n. p.)--a very famous name

116. hypercoaster (n.)--a roller-coaster that is said to reach new heights in its use of thrills

117. in a heartbeat (prep. p)--very quickly; very suddenly

118. in the black (prep. n.) - To be out of big trouble.

(prep. n.)--To be out of debt; to be under budget; to be out of a financial deficit.

119. in the red (prep. n.)--To be in a lot of trouble.

(prep. n.)--To be in a lot of debt; to be over budget; to be in a financial deficit.

120. in the zone (prep. n.)--To be in a certain "high"(due to adrenalin or other motivations).

(prep. n.)--To be inside a certain line or boundary in a sporting court or rink.

(prep. n.)--To be at the target heart rate (or near it) during exercise.

121. J (n.) - In basketball, a "jumper"; a jump shot.

122. Jack and Jill (v. p.)--a ballroom dance competition (or other dance competition)

where partners are selected at random

123. jack (v.)--To hijack a car; to carjack

(v.)--To shoot a firearm (especially, a gun)

124. jack up (v.)--To raise (prices).

(v.)--To raise one number to a new number.

125. jam (n.)--An imbroglio; a confusion

(n.)--In basketball, a slam dunk.

126. jammage (n.)--refers to the word 'jam', a pitcher's technique of throwing a bail so fast that the batter won't have time to hit the ball with the meat of the bat at the right time, keeping the ball in the ball park (baseball)

127. jam sandwich (n.)--same as the word 'jammage' (baseball)

(n.)--A gridlock of any kind.

128. jive (v.) To dance to swing music.

(v.) To dance in a very jovial, often improvised (and lively) fashion.

(v.) To do a jazz-style jam session.

(n.) Swing and/or jazz music.

129. John (n.) - This refers to a police officer who pretends to be a prostitute (doing undercover work) to a person who wishes to pay money for he/she to have sex with that person. The one who pays the money is then usually arrested by surprise and usually charged with either prostitution or solicitation of prostitution. Therefore, A John (or Johns) are usually used in anti-prostitution sting by police.

130. joyride (n.)- This involves a person (usually an adolescent or other juvenile) who, after stealing a vehicle with or without force, rides it just for the pleasure of loving the vehicle in the first place.

131. jump bail (v.) To avoid or refuse to appear in court to avoid a subpoena for a criminal trial (if required of the arrestee of the crime).

132. jump the tracks (v.)--to derail (usu. happens to a train).

133. junkie (n.)--a foolish person; a person who loves to eat junk food

134. kaplooie! (n.)--another way of saying 'kaboom!'

135. Kosovar (adj.)--a person native of Kosovo (an area in Yugoslavia)

136. laser-guided (adj.)--often said of a bomb or a missile that uses laser technology to guide such weapons to the target

137. lay-up (n.) - This basketball shot is usually done in the free-throw lane, where the offender jumps, and during the jump, he releases the ball with his outstretched hand that releases it.

138. leading lady (n. p.) - A lady or woman in television, theater, or music who plays a major or very major role.

139. legwork (n.)--hard work

140. light-speed (adj.)--very fast; very quick

141. liner (n.)--in baseball, a nickname for a line drive

142. live large (v. p.)--to live overweight or obese

143. live from paycheck to paycheck (v. p.)--To deal with getting only a wage to support oneself financially with at least a considerable fear of not having job security or the fear of being fired or laid off.

144. Lolita (n.) - Literally meaining "Little Lola" in Spanish, it refers to a lady who loves to have sex with anyone under the statutory age (of consent). It was probably inspired by Nabokov's novel based on the same name.

145 - loose cannon (n. p.) - This refers to someone who can explode into great craziness, humor, or even anger at almost any time.

146. low (adj.)--indication of something starting to break down, wear down, or rot

147. lowdown (n.)--events or anything else happening right now

148. make out (v. p.) - To have sex or sexual intercourse in bed or in a vehicle.

149. make some noise (v. p.)--to become famous; to start being noticed

150. make waves (v. p.)--to start being attractive or famous

151. mass grave (n. p.)--a gravesite that is usually makeshift and buries hundreds of people, often happening during war

152. mass e-mail (n. p.)--any e-mail message that has a lot of bandwidth in it

153. majorly (adj.)--dearly

154. media circus (n. p.)--This means a situation where a celebrity or public person is hounded by media personnel (paparazzi or not) for the purpose of making this person have a big effect or result on future outcomes or reputation.

155. mom-and-pop (adj.)--This refers to a small business or, more distinctly, a store or business run by a single family.

156. motor (v.)--to move; to go in motion; to speed

157. narcotrafficker (n.)--A narcotics trafficker, especially those in the country of Colombia.

(n.)--A drug dealer or trafficker (of illicit drugs) who is known or notorious for ruthlessness.

158. netter (n.)--volleyball player

159. newbie (n.)--Someone trying out a new thing one has never done before.

(n.) - A tyro.

(n.) - A new class member or new student.

160. Nicad (n.)--acroynm for nickel-cadnium battery

161. nitty-gritty (colloq. n.)--basics

162. no-trespass (adj.) - A type of order (usually a legal one) ordering a person a person not to enter and/or come near a place or establishment indefinitely.

163. nod (n.)--acceptance (of an offer)

164. off the hook (prep. n.) - Free from any possible penalty, punishmnent, sentence, or other chastisement imposed.

(prep. n.) - Free from responsibility.

165. off the glass (prep. n.) - In basketball, a shot that hits the glass area of the backboard before it goes into the basket.

166. oldies (n.)--music, mainly pop, of the past

167. on the beat (prep. n.) - This refers to a police officer walking a round assigned to him (a block, street, etc.) in order to enforce the law.

166. one lump sum (prep. n.) - This means that one wants any sweepstakes or lottery winnings, court settlement damages, or wage earnings to be sent to the person in the whole amount--not just in installments or in partial payments.

167. overpriced (adj.)--inflated (in price); expensive

168. pack (v.)--to fill up

169. paint (n.) - In basketball, the colored area (usually dark) that indicates the free throw area of the court.

170. pair of balls (pl.n.)—testicles

171. pat-down (adj.) This is a type of security search on a person (usually done by a police officer, security guard, or a corrections officer) to see if illicit drugs or weapons can be felt on that person.

172. penetrate (v.)--to go through the defenders (basketball)

173. Philly (n.) A nickname of a person who lives in Philadelphia (in the U.S.)

   (n.) A Philadelphia Phillies baseball player.

174. picture-perfect (adj.)--perfect to one's liking or choosing

175. port-a-potty (n.)--portable bathroom

176. potty (n.)--bathroom

177. power alleys (c.n.)--areas of the wall on left-center and right-center outfield areas (baseball)

178. price-out (v.)--to avoid purchasing an item because of an inflation or increase in its price

179. pump strength (v. p.)--to give strength to something; to create or build strength

180. pump up (v. p.)--to shoot (basketball); to raise something

181. pussy (n.)—skin; sex

182. pyro-spectacular (n.)--fireworks show (or display)

183. Quad (n.)--nickname for the quadrangle, a common outside landscape in some universities

184. raging bull (n. p.)--an angry person; a person who gets easily angered, usually with explosive behavior

185. railroad (v.)--to frame someone; to blame and punish someone too swiftly by reason of impatience, fear, or overzealousness

186. reach base (v.)--to go safely to a base by menas of a hit or a walk

187. real-world (adj.)--actual; real

188. real world (n. p.)--the reality of life

189. run (n.)--a situation where a team is on a winning streak in the game by shooting opportunistic baskets due to an opposing team's turnovers, missed shots, etc.

190. run (v.)--to be ejected; to be thrown out

VARIANT: run the plates (v.)--a police check on a driver's license plate for any outstanding driving infractions

191. sacked (adj.)--referred to the bases being loaded, such as bases sacked (baseball);

(adj.)--also, a quarterback being tackled by a defender way behind the former person's line of scrimmage (football)

192. save a bundle (v. p.)—to save plenty; to save a lot

193. schlew (n.)--crowd

194. scum (n.)--a dirty film usually on the shower windows

195. score big (v. p.)--to make a greatly positive change or happening

196. shoot pool (v. p.)--to play billiards

197. sista (n.)--sister

198. skip (n.)--manager (baseball)

199. skip town (v. p.)--to leave town; to flee or run out of town

200. slip-and-fall (n. p.)--short for 'slip-and-fall accident'

201. smoker (n.)--smoke grenade

202. sortie (n.)--In war, a bombing or reconnisance mission by a military aircraft

203. spank (v.)--to make a team suffer a very humiliating defeat

204. spiker (n.)--volleyball player

205. split-second (adj.)--very quick

206. stage (v.)--to make something seem as if is going to be real, often to create a scam or to collect money deceivingly

207. storms (pl. n.) - Referred to as a nickname for "thunderstorms".

208. street rod (n. p.)--a modified vehicle, often with silver-coated tailpipes, often used for illegal drag racing.

209. submission hold (n. p.) - In free-fight wrestling, a wrestler who executes a hold (on an opposing wrestler) that is so painful that the opposing wrestler has no choice but to give up and close the match.

(n. p.) - In the martial arts (including jujitsu and karate), it is a hold or grab intended to subdue an aggressor in real-life situations (in order to try to counteract the "aggression" on the agressor).

210. suck (v.)--a disapproving reaction to bad or horrible conditions

211. swing for the fences (v. p.)--to hit a home run (baseball)

212. stench (n.)--ugly odor

213. sting (v.)--to defeat a team painfully

214. stinko (n.)--person who stinks

215. sugar (n.)--sweetheart; pretty lady

216. tagger (n.)--a leader or main part of a gang who writes grafitti

217. take a toll (v. p.)--to suffer; endure hardship or damaging stress

218. take the stand (v.)--to go up on the witness stand (in a courtroom)

219. tater (n.)--home run

220. thanks a bunch (colloq.)--thanks a lot

221. thanx (colloq.)--thanks

222. thou (n.)--A nickname for 'thousand' when referring to prices

223. thou (prn.)--'you (are)'

224. thousands (n.)--thousands of people, places of things; thousands of dollars

225. threesome (n.)--an interplay (usually sexual or erotic) involving three persons

226. tie the knot (v. p.) - To get married; to get betrothed.

(v. p.) - To go to a wedding place (or church) to exchange wedding vows (between husband and wife).

227. tit (n.)--one of the two ball-like protrusions on either side of the breast

228. hit the three (v.)--to shoot a 3-point shot (basketball)

229. to play by the rules (v.)--to follow rules or regulations

230. toss (v.)--to eject; expel

231. turf (n.) - A nickname for artificial turf on football, baseball, soccer, and tennis

fields.

(n.) - A street gang territory that the gangsters rule; a set.

(n.) - A boundary.

232. turn off (v.)--to keep someone from making contact with another person

233. turn on (v.)--to arouse someone to make contact with another person

234. two-bagger (n.)--double (baseball)

235. under the gun (prep. p.) - To be under the possible threat or danger of harm, damage, injury, or death.

(prep. p.) - To be threatened with possible or imminent violent weather or violent storms.

236. unstain (v.)--to get rid of or remove the stain

237. uphill battle (n. p.)--a different battle

238. upper tank (n. [/)--upper deck (baseball)

239. waiting to exhale (g. p.) - Made famous by the famous 1997 movie involving 4 Black middle-aged single women, it means a situation when a person is expecting a great, full, love life when he or she realizes instead that it is even harder due to high expectations on relationships.

(g.p.) - To expect something that will enrich that person very happily.

240. wallop (v.)--to make a team suffer a humiliating defeat

241. wan' (colloq.)--a contraction of 'want'.

242. want out (v. p.)--to release oneself from an obbligation, duty, homework, or errand

243. wardead (n.)--those soldiers who died in war or combat

244. whaler (n.)--a hunter who hunts for and/or kills whales

245. whip (v.)--to defeat an opposing team by making it score the fewest points

246. wire (n.)--the finish line in a horse race

247. world-class (adj.)--the best; great

248. yard (n.)--ballpark; a recreational area in a jail or prison

249. yep! (interj.) – something like an affirmation, as if you are really saying "yes"

250. Zs (pl.) – sleep time

BIOGRAPHY

Charles Joseph Smith, who was born and raised in Chicago, started his adventure in creative writing somewhere in the 1980s when his mother encouraged him to write journals about his life, when word came out that Charles had autism spectrum disorder. Gradually, over the years, as he was being a musical savant, his writing interest grew soon after his teenage years, starting off with composing his own original structured poems, and then freeform poems, as well as some short stories, and then resorting to a few musical scripts to his own music.

While he was attending the University of Illinois at Urbana-Champaign, Charles' writing interests skyrocketed when he befriended a small group called The Red Herring Poets in Urbana, IL, where Carmen Pursifull, herself a established independent writer, took charge. He used his participation in the poetic group to write a number of original poems to be critiqued. His interest in poetic writing helped him achieve a passing grade in the English 101—Introduction to Poetry class with Brian O'Broin. Also during that campus stay, several of his original poems made the semi-finals in the National Library of Poetry contests, including "My Music Fills Me With A Flair" (1997) and "My Beautiful Piano Fingers" (1999). Another of his poems, "Out of the Abyss of Sorrow", appeared in the National Library of Poetry's compilation, The Isle of View, and also got the Editors' Choice Award from the National Library of Poetry in 1997, and in the same year, another of his poems, "My Music Kills My Pain", made the finals in the National Library of Poetry contests. Also at the same campus, he joined up with the Newspoets, an online organization featuring poems of political satire or humor, made up of some members from the School of Designing a Society, a permacultural group. Near the end of his campus stay, Charles successfully wrote a doctoral dissertation which turned into a reduced lecture-recital script about several of Franz Liszt's operatic transcriptions, at the University of Illinois at Urbana-Champaign from 1995 to 2002. It was eventually published in the IDEALS Repository at the campus.

Charles' gifts in writing allowed him to compose his own first website using PageMill 2.0, and, having achieved assimilation in the rise of Internet technology, was able to do some writing topics on the dancing-discuss-1 threads when he was part of the Dancing Illini of the University of Illinois. He also tried his hand in screenwriting, trying to compose a dance movie script called "Salsa, Merengue, and Obsession" due to his love of ballroom and Latin dancing, but the project fell under and is under hiatus due to unyielding academic and musical commitments.

His postdoctoral life did not mean an end to his writing. When meeting up with Lynn West, who co-founded the Celebration of Joy Inc., Lynn's awareness of Charles' autism encouraged him to write an autobiography, which was published on Amazon.com, but now is on hold because he plans to add more material and is doing more editing. He also wrote scores of original new material on Blogger.com, and is using the Internet writing board, Quora, to answer questions on writing and music. He also recently joined up with the new Internet writing platform, wikiHow, where he published several new articles.

www.ingramcontent.com/pod-product-compliance
Lightning Source LLC
Chambersburg PA
CBHW020332290526
45785CB00007B/3032